HOW TO

PROPHESY

"Pursue love, and earnestly desire the spiritual gifts, especially that you may prophesy."

1 CORINTHIANS 14:1 (ESV)

Written by Kay Nash

ACKNOWLEDGEMENTS

Was it not for my husband Ryan (Timothy) Nash, I would not be where I am today. This book would not be possible without his hours of work behind the scenes. Whether through editing or cover design, he always helps keep this train moving. He is my rock, my best friend and my love, and nothing, I repeat, nothing in this ministry would happen without him. I dedicate this book to him who gave my prophetic ministry wings. An anointing without money, time or people is only beneficial to a few, but two can send ten thousand.

To my family, who sacrificed for my future constantly. I love you and you are what keeps me going in times when I want to give up.

To Anna, my assistant. Without her prayers and encouragement, I don't know where I would be. During the writing of this book she was the intercessor that this ministry needed, and she helped us pray through many obstacles. I am forever thankful for her prayers and love in this season. She will be headed out to California soon, but her season with us was of great benefit.

To all our ministry partners who have stuck by us financially every month, whether we are on TV, Radio, YouTube, writing books or traveling, many of you have supported it all. You are the backbone of this ministry and I am grateful for you.

For those of you who have purchased all of my books, thank you. I hope you are as blessed by this one as you were the others. For those of you new to this ministry, welcome! I hope this book is a blessing to you and sows new wisdom into your life.

"For wisdom is far more valuable than rubies. Nothing you desire can compare with it."
Proverbs 8:11 (NLT)

As you read this book, I want you to take it seriously. If you can do that, you will find keys to unlock the prophetic gift inside you. For those of you who are already operating in this gift, I pray you will see deep truths that are often hidden. Wherever you are at in your journey, there are many take-aways from this book. This is a very practical book; if you do the things it says you will see results. We have trained many people in the prophetic and helped people go from barely hearing God for themselves to prophesying over others. These tips will work if you apply to them to your life. If you want answers about the prophetic, they are in this book. There will be stories, tips, biblical theology training and much more. You will be able to prophesy after reading this book, if you open your mouth and speak what He tells you. Are you ready? Let's learn about the prophetic!

TABLE OF CONTENTS

INTRODUCTION

The bible tells us to be hungry for the prophetic. In fact, it tells us to lust after it, and it even says to lust after it above all spiritual gifts. Why? Because it can help God's people get to where they are supposed to go. My hope is that you will understand that the prophetic exists to help people. By learning about it, you are going to be able to help more people who are confused get clear on what God is saying, or hope for things they never could have even dreamed up.

One time I prophesied something so big over a guy in one of my meetings that he could barely handle it. It was so outside his normal way of thinking that he could hardly comprehend that *he* could do something so amazing.

The prophetic is awesome, as it helps people fly higher with God and get past their insecure self-images to believe for something more. And let's be honest, it is simply cool to know what God is saying for people.

For the last five and a half years I have done just that, delivering prophecies to thousands of individuals around the world, and training others to prophesy as well. It has been a wild ride of us all getting to know God more and believing for things we never thought possible.

For three of those years I have taught Prophetic Ministry Schools for women in Florida, working with the ladies for twelve weeks at a time. While doing this, we started receiving applications from people all over the world who wanted to come, but couldn't because of how far away they lived from us or because their schedule just wouldn't allow. Upon trying to deal with this, I decided writing a book would be a good way to go. That way, no matter the time or location, you can get trained in the prophetic. My hope is that this book helps people all over who wanted training from me in the prophetic, and that it also helps people new to this ministry strengthen their gift.

For those of you who have already received prophetic training from me, there are some new revelations in here as well, so don't zone out!

So why would I share my process and keys with you? Why not keep all this knowledge to myself?

Quite simply, because I cannot prophesy over every person in the whole world. But I believe together as a collective we can all do our part in delivering the word of God to the people around us. We all have an area of influence, whether at the office, at your church or even with your children, there is someone you can share God's heart with. My goal is not to exalt myself but rather to exalt you into a position of one who can prophesy, and one who can prophesy accurately.

I also wrote this book because I don't see a lot of prophets teaching on how to operate in the prophetic. They offer you vague generalities but don't give you the meat. My desire is that this book would be meat. You won't get a bunch of concepts about prophecy, but rather biblical truth with the Holy Spirit guiding you into all knowledge in the matter. There will also be practical application from my own experiences. My hope is that whether you call yourself a prophet/prophetess, or you just want to strengthen your gift, this book will help you. Even if you don't understand the prophetic at all, this book can still help you.

Why should you care about prophecy?

Well, you must understand that when you prophesy you are speaking for Jesus. The more we can speak His words in this world, the more the world will become like Him. Prophecy is not declaring a thought that one thinks is good. Prophecy is repeating the exact words God said to you, in order to encourage, equip or correct someone or a group into what God is calling them to do.

I do not subscribe to the theology that you can never correct people with prophecy. I figured I needed to address this now, before some of you are confused. I find no biblical basis for this, as there are many corrections and directions in the bible. If you are okay with being open to this thought, this book will be very helpful to you.

I love you, and my hope is that you see my heart is to teach you so well that you don't need me to prophesy for you, but rather you are able to prophesy over others and encourage them. That when I, or another prophet, prophesies over you it will serve more as a confirmation as you become very in tune with Him.

May you enjoy this book and be educated and edified. Please teach anyone you can these truths. They are not mine to hoard but yours to share.

I love you.

Your Messenger,

Kay Nash

CHAPTER 1

WHAT IS PROPHECY, AND IS IT FOR NOW OR LATER?

To understand the gift of prophecy we must first understand what prophecy is *not*. The reason I say this is because there are a lot of things going around that are pretending to be prophecy, and I need to address them first so you can have your mind clear and not be deceived by these things.

These "nots" have hurt the church and others outside the church for many years. After we go through this list, we will dive into what prophecy really is, so you are able to make a distinction.

WHAT PROPHECY IS *NOT*

To be successful in prophesying over others, yourself, or any group of people, you must understand this statement:

Just because you have a good thought, even in a church building, doesn't mean it is Godly prophetic thought.

I have seen this false belief manifest many times in Christian meetings. A group will be praying together and someone will get a true word from the Lord, and then someone else will be *"compelled"* to share a thought they had directly after the person sharing the real Word of the Lord. They assume it must also be God because they are in church and someone is prophesying, so it must be divine revelation, right? Possibly not. Just because you have a thought in a church, even in a prophetic, Holy Spirit moving meeting, does not mean it is from God. When you allow this truth to saturate your soul you will realize that lots of thoughts try to masquerade as prophecy, but they are just some thoughts, or in worse cases, demons. But we will get into that later.

Even nice thoughts, without the Holy Spirit saying them, are just thoughts.

We must remember these two things: Our heart can be deceitful among all things (Jeremiah 17:9), and when it is not healed our thoughts are not always Godly, no matter the environment.

"The heart is deceitful above all things, and desperately wicked; who can know it? I, the Lord, search the heart; I test the mind to reward a man according to his way, by what his deeds deserve."
Jeremiah 17:9-10 (KJV & BSB)

So sometimes we can "prophesy" out of our heart and not know it. Check out this verse:

"How long shall this be in the heart of the prophets that prophesy lies? yea, they are prophets of the deceit of their own heart"
Jeremiah 23:26 (KJV)

Sometimes the devil would like nothing better than to throw us off during a church meeting. I don't say this to make you paranoid, but think about it; if the devil spoke to you in church it may be harder for you to accept that it was the devil speaking. You would say "Well I was in church and I heard this voice, so it must have been God." Not necessarily. Of course God does speak while you are in church, but a thought you have is not always prophecy or God. Every spirit, no matter where it is, must be tested. You must also consider the question, who is talking to you? Remember the enemy comes to steal, kill and destroy, and he does so pretending to be an angel of light. So not every encounter, even if it seemingly good, is an encounter from God.

"The thief does not come except to steal, and to kill, and to destroy..."
John 10:10 (NKJV)

"Satan disguises himself as an angel of light."
2 Corinthians 11:14 (ESV)

One of the worst manifestations of this I see going around is marriage assumptions. If you are honest, most likely you or someone you know has thought that God "told them" to marry someone that wasn't actually who God has for them. This isn't a bad thing; the desire to marry someone is a good desire. However, the desire to marry the wrong person may come from the devil, and we need to understand this as well.

Just because something is good doesn't mean it is God. We must test the spirits to discern if it is God.

For over five years of my life I served as a Prophetic Life Coach for women; helping them know God, heal their hearts and walk in their destinies. Many women would come in with all sorts of questions and thoughts and alleged "words from God" about marrying a man. I am going to share a few situations to help you understand this concept more.

One girl I was overseeing told me that "God had told her" she was supposed to marry a certain man. I asked her what the guy she was interested in had to say about that thought. She told me she hadn't spoken to him about the matter. I told her to see if he felt the same way, as a prophetic word like that would need mutual agreement. Sadly, he was not interested in her and ended up marrying someone else. This was heartbreaking for her, but the truth of the matter is stories like this happens all the time.

With prophetic words involving others, you need to make sure that they are on the same page as you before moving toward that word. Otherwise it can be merely chasing a fantasy, and the devil would like nothing more than to get you stuck in a fantasy that is never going to manifest. The bible tells us that chasing fantasies makes no sense:

"A hard worker has plenty of food, but a person who chases fantasies has no sense."
Proverbs 12:11 (NLT)

Many people chase fantasies, as they don't know how to tell the difference between their heart, the devil, and God. People often think that just because it's a good thing, means it is God. The devil uses these "good", but not Godly, thoughts to waste your time when you could be pursuing the things God really has for you.

Some versions of the scripture I mentioned above say chasing fantasies leads to poverty. I also like that version, because it means when you chase fantasies you get nothing. Many in our time are chasing fantasies in relationships that the devil is disguising as prophetic words. It is truly sad the ground that the devil has in this area, but I believe with proper prophetic training you can make the right choice for yourself. You may even mentor someone else into the right path, so that their words from the Lord manifest.

The opposite can also be true if a person has wrong views of God. Another woman I was coaching told me that God had told her that she was supposed to marry her former husband who was abusive. I said that was interesting, and I asked her to ask this "voice" that told her that if Jesus Christ has come in the flesh. I then explained to her that a voice from God should confess that Jesus Christ has come in the flesh when asked (I will go more in to this teaching later on). So she asked the voice that told her to marry an abusive man, "Has Jesus Christ come in the flesh?" The voice said "No!" She was freaked out and realized that a demon had pretended to be God and tricked her into marrying her abusive former husband. She had already left him at the time, so I am thankful that this revelation did not cause craziness. But it did bring her peace to know that God would not want her to be beat.

You must understand that demons can lie and pretend to be God.

Demons can lie and say they are from God when they are not. The devil has no problem pretending to be God. Remember, it was satan's pride that had him go start his own team against God.

Whole false doctrines and religions have started from someone hearing a voice that was "God", "an Angel" or "Jesus". Often, the problem is not that they didn't hear a voice, but that they just believed the voice without any testing of it. We can see in the above verses we talked about before that we are told in the Bible to test the spirits, but sadly people often do not do this, and just believe any voice they hear. This causes grave error in the prophetic. You can sometimes go into a church and the whole church is hearing the wrong voice, but since everyone is hearing the same voice, they are all in agreement and it is hard to convince them otherwise. It is kind of a scary thought, but the same demon can talk to all these people so they are all in agreement, but that doesn't mean what they are believing is God. Do yourself a favor and test the spirits to make sure.

I know that testing the spirits is often taught as just making sure it lines up with the word of God. Though that is okay on the surface, as you go further into your walk, the devil will try to trip you up with scripture verses, much like he did with Jesus when He was in the wilderness.

"Then the devil took Him up into the holy city, set Him on the pinnacle of the temple, and said to Him, "If You are the Son of God, throw Yourself down. For it is written: 'He shall give His angels charge over you,' and, 'In their hands they shall bear you up, lest you dash your foot against a stone.'"
Matthew 4:5 (NKJV)

See here how the devil quotes scripture to try to convince Jesus to do something wrong? He says "It is written" and then quotes a verse from the Old Testament in Psalm 91:11-12. The devil was trying to use scripture to cause Jesus to sin. Obviously Jesus did not fall for it because He knows the sound of His master's voice, and God was not anointing this scripture verse for Him for now.

Just because it is scripture doesn't mean it is prophecy. Scripture must be anointed by God to become prophetic.

We cannot just pull any scripture verse out and call it prophecy. The Holy Spirt must anoint it. This is maturity. People have gone around shouting scripture verses until they are blue in the face and nothing has manifested because the verse was not anointed for them for now. You need to ask God if this verse is for you for now. If it is, then by all means declare it till you see it manifest. But if not, ask God which verse is for you for now. Also be open to it not being what you want. This can be hard, but having a soft heart that wants God's will more than your own desires will help you be more accurate with sharing prophetic words.

Prophecy is not necessarily "wisdom" from past experiences.

I have seen this happen too many times in the church where a young woman or girl will want advice on what she is supposed to do in a situation. An older woman will tell her "Well I got a prophetic word for you. When I was your age this happened to me too and this is what I did, so this is what you should do." Umm? What part of that is prophetic? Just because you may have been in the exact same situation, doesn't mean that person is supposed to do the exact same thing.

We must understand that two people going through the exact same situation may have two different solutions to their problems. The prophetic is not a formula. The prophetic is individual.

Prophecy is also not just saying things you want to happen in Jesus' name. Though the name of Jesus is powerful, you can't just use it to get anything you want. Sometimes Jesus says no to you.

A child in the spirit runs around declaring things that they want to happen. A mature

person in the spirit says what God says, eventually putting their own will aside for His will.

Jesus followed God to the death. He didn't just run around screaming His will. Rather, He laid down his life for the will of God. We must be like Jesus.

This doesn't mean God does not care about your desires, as the Bible says "Delight in the Lord and He will give you the desires of your heart." This means God wants to give you your desires, but sometimes the timing of them or the way they manifest may be different than what you thought. You need to be open to this.

WHAT PROPHECY *IS*

Okay now that we got some things out of the way that are not prophecy, what *is* prophecy?

Prophecy, quite simply, is the testimony of Jesus. We see this in the book of Revelation:

"And I fell at his feet to worship him. But he said to me, "See that you do not do that! I am your fellow servant, and of your

*brethren who have the testimony of Jesus. Worship God! **For the testimony of Jesus is the spirit of prophecy.**"*
Revelation 19:10 (NKJV)

So what does that mean practically? Prophecy is what Jesus would like to testify about. In other words, when we prophesy over a person, nation or business we are testifying to what Jesus would like to say to them.

Prophecy is used to tell of future events that Jesus says will happen. It helps encourage the person and direct them on the course God has for them and sometimes it corrects them.

*"But he that prophesies speaks **edification** and **exhortation** and **comfort** to men."*
1 Corinthians 14:3 (NKJV)

The bible lists here 3 things that prophecy does: Edifies, Exhorts and Comforts.

Some of you will cringe right now as these will not be put in order, respectively. However, this is the very nature of the prophetic. Put things in His order. Not what makes sense.

Let's break these apart in the Greek so you can understand what they mean.

Comforts: The word used here is *paramythia.* Paramythia means any address, whether made for the purpose of persuading, or of arousing and stimulating, or of calming and consoling

Edifies: The word here is oikodomēhe. It means the act of one who promotes another's growth in Christian wisdom, piety, happiness, holiness.

I want you to note here that it says holiness. Part of prophecy is to promote someone's holiness. To do this, there are times you will have to correct them or direct them on a different path that leads them into more holiness. Yes, we are holy by the blood of Jesus when we stand before the throne, but that doesn't mean we should allow our flesh to do whatever it wants; this is sin. Jesus lived a sinless life, and though we may never be sinless per-say, we can continue to be sanctified as we rid our lives of certain sins.

Exhorts: The word here is paraklēsis. This word has many meanings, so I will try to create a small summary here. It means: exhortation, admonition, encouragement. It also means to have "persuasive discourse" which can also mean to correct.

Essentially, the prophetic is supposed to help your brother or sister in the Lord become more whole, well and holy. It is also supposed to increase their happiness. Remember, the truth sets free. It is better to tell someone the truth because it will ultimately lead to their happiness later, for holiness leads to peace in the long run.

Holiness is the hard part of prophecy. This refining process is hard but there is a reward. The more God can trust you, the more He can give you. In the prophetic we also get to tell people about their future and what God has called them to do. This is rewarding and fun.

BALANCED PROPHECY

As you can see above, prophecy is correction, edification, direction, etc. It is many things, but ultimately it is for the betterment of the person.

Prophecy is supposed to be balanced.

But we often see that some prophets/ prophetic ministries seem to go one way or the other. Some "prophets" only prophesy doom and gloom all the time, while other "prophets" only prophesy hope and everything working out. It should be both. Now, I put the word prophets in quotes because some of these people are indeed imposters, where others are just oblivious and others rebellious. Let the Holy Spirit show you which is which.

We must understand there are still times where the judgement of God is at hand. We see the judgment of God many times in the Bible. But there are times where God is sharing the joy and good things coming. So why do people just seem to hang out in one camp? Often times they are broken.

One side of the prophetic camp refuses to give or receive any rebukes. The other side goes too far, seeing God only as a fiery judge because maybe they have only seen pain in their life, or have another spirit talking to them. I have seen the judgment of God in my life as the Lord ripped apart churches that came against me. But I have also seen the grace of God in my life that healed me from an STD that I deserved to have. I had sex outside the covenant of marriage and I was stained from it, but God in His grace healed me supernaturally. I know a God who is full of grace and justice all at the same time. I know some of you don't want to embrace the judgement side of God and I get it. But God isn't abusive, He is just.

Say a sex trafficker who has trafficked thousands of women, and is unrepentant, is locked up for the rest of his life. Is this not just? On the other hand, let's say a girl has sex outside of marriage once, or gets drunk one night because she is looking for love and doesn't know the love of God. Wouldn't it make sense that God would send her loving people who care about her so she can know God and experience His love rather than punishing her? God knows people's hearts; we do not. However, God can show us people's hearts through the prophetic.

Things are not always black and white in the prophetic. They are often gray.

The sooner you understand this the better. Every situation is different, and you must respond the way God wants to respond, rather than in a formulaic way. Although two people can do the same thing, the heart motive may be different. God looks at the heart and not the action.

Some people simply do not know the difference between right and wrong, or how to stop even if they do, whereas other people just want to be evil. We have all seen an addict who cannot get clean but just loves everyone they meet. But we have also all seen an angry person who cares about no one but themselves. Glean the difference in people's hearts from the Holy Ghost's promptings.

If you want to ever be successful at prophecy, never assume anything!

Be humble and simply ask God what He wants to say to a person.

If you don't know how to Hear God's voice, I would suggest reading my book Hearing God for Yourself, where I go in depth on how to hear God accurately. But to save those who read that book already, I will not do a full teaching in this book.

IS PROPHECY FOR NOW?

I have been hearing lately that many people believe prophecy is not for now, and that scripture is the only prophecy. These people often have a mentality of, "We are just waiting for

Jesus to come back to hear words from God again." This is unbiblical and a demonic thought process. This belief stops God's children from knowing what their father is saying to them intimately, which is the very thing Jesus died for. One of the reasons Jesus died was to reconcile us back to the father. Sadly, the belief in a lack of prophecy for now stops people from knowing God, their father, in an intimate way. This intimate God wants to tell His children things for their future and the futures of others. Why? Because He wants to give them thorough understanding and comfort while walking out their destinies. The more you know about your future, the more you can be at peace.

Think about it this way; let's say God tells you for example that you're going to lose your job and that He has another path for you. As a result, when your boss tells you that you're fired, you would be more at ease because you already knew it was coming. It may still hurt, but it wouldn't hurt as bad because Jesus told you already.

"Surely the Lord GOD will do nothing,
but he revealeth his secret unto his
servants the prophets."
Amos 3:7 (KJV)

Scripture also shows us how prophecy is for now, so let's check it out below in Acts 2:14-17:

"Then Peter stood up with the Eleven, raised his voice and addressed the crowd: "Fellow Jews and all of you who live in Jerusalem, let me explain this to you; listen carefully to what I say. These people are not drunk, as you suppose. It's only nine in the morning! But this is that which was spoken by the prophet Joel: 'In the last days, God says, I will pour out my Spirit on all people. Your sons and daughters will prophesy, your young men will see visions, your old men will dream dreams.'"
Acts 2:14-17 (NIV)

There is more, but let's break this down first. We see that Peter is addressing a crowd right after Pentecost, where we know that speaking in tongues fell. It created such a commotion that Peter had to tell people what was going on as they were confused. He tells them that what is happening is from a prophecy given by the Prophet Joel in the old testament. What he is referring to here is a prophecy that Joel gave in Joel 2:28 which says:

"And it shall come to pass afterward that I will pour out my spirit upon all flesh; and your sons and your daughters shall prophesy, your old men shall dream dreams, your young men shall see visions."
Joel 2:28 (NKJV)

Okay so what he is saying here is that Joel prophesied about a time where God would pour out His Spirit on all flesh, and this prophecy was taking place on that very day: Pentecost. The prophecy goes on to say that this outpouring will allow sons and daughters to prophesy, meaning that men and women can prophesy. It then says young men shall see visions, meaning young people can see visions and prophesy, and that old men will dream dreams, meaning old people can receive prophetic downloads as well.

So what we just learned here is that Joel prophesied about a time when all flesh would prophesy, regardless of age, gender or social class, and that it started at Pentecost. And I believe it is still happening now. There is no scriptural evidence that I can find that says this outpouring has stopped. Rejoice, you can prophesy!

CHAPTER 2

WHO CAN PROPHESY, AND ARE YOU A PROPHET?

I hope you discovered in the last chapter that *you* can prophesy, whether man or woman, young or old, or rich or poor. God can use you to speak life into someone by relating what Jesus wants to say to them. Never disqualify yourself. If God can speak through a donkey, can He not speak through you? You, who are much better than a donkey. You have been bought at a price; the blood of His Son. Don't disqualify yourself. You are fearfully and wonderfully made.

It's doesn't matter age, gender or social status, all God's children can prophesy thanks to the outpouring at Pentecost.

Another lie I hear going through the church is that there were once prophets in the old testament, but now in the new testament there is not a need for prophets.

I am going to try not to get worked up here, but this is just not scriptural at all, and is another lie from the devil! There are prophets listed in the New Testament for sure. Anna the prophetess is a perfect example of this. We will go more into her story below. She prophesies about Jesus while He is right near her. I am pretty sure if this was a sin, we would have known about it by now. There are other prophets mentioned in the new testament as well, so for education's sake, I will tell you some of the new testament prophets. But before I go into that, I want to make something else clear:

WOMEN CAN PROPHESY!

Again, Anna is a good example here. Anna is an often-overlooked prophetess in the new testament, as many women have been told women cannot speak in the church. Honestly this makes no sense, though it makes sense why people would think that when reading certain scripture verses. However, the fact that there is even the term *"prophetess"* in the bible means that woman can speak for God. There are references to this title in the new and old testaments; we see Huldah and Deborah as prophetesses in the old testament, and Anna and the four virgin daughters in the new testament. The thought that women cannot speak for God is an absolutely bizarre and sexist lie the devil has come up with to stop certain words of God from coming forth and to bind woman. I just want to make it really clear what I and God think about this matter. He did not die so women could be more bound then they were before He came.

Now, you may be thinking, "But didn't Paul say certain women couldn't speak in the church?" First off, yes, Paul did say that. Keep in mind though that Paul said it, not Jesus. We have a problem in the American church of acting like Paul was basically Jesus. Jesus never bound women, He loosed them. Second, that was to a specific people group, not to everyone of all time. We have to be careful of taking a certain scripture verse and making it an all-time truth, when other verses (such as the ones that speak about the several women prophetesses I mentioned above) contradict that. When there seems to be a contradiction in scripture you must seek the Holy Spirit and ask His thought on the matter. I am so confident in this that I encourage you to go ahead and ask God if women can speak in His church yourself. You may be surprised at the freedom this brings. Sorry if this seems like a rant, but some of you need to hear this in order to get unbound from this religious thinking, so you can be the bold woman you are supposed to be. Study prophetesses in the Bible if you want to put an end to this once and for all.

Okay now that that is out of the way, let's jump into some new testament prophets so you can have examples:

SOME NEW TESTAMENT PROPHETS

John the Baptist

Even though John said he was not a prophet, Jesus refers to him as such and more than that, a Messenger.

Anna the Praying Prophetess

Anna the prophetess was a widow who prayed often and was constantly in the house of God. She had the honor of being there when Jesus was presented to the Lord, and prophesied about His life.

"And there was one Anna, a prophetess, the daughter of Phanuel, of the tribe of Aser: she was of great age..."
Luke 2:36 (KJV)

The four virgins Prophetesses

"Now this man had four virgin daughters who were prophetesses."
Acts 21:9 (NASB)

SOME OLD TESTAMENT PROPHETS

Deborah the Prophetess

Deborah was an old testament prophetess who helped judge and free Israel from cruel bondage by Sisera. She was also a married woman.

"Now Deborah, a prophetess, the wife of Lappidoth, was judging Israel at that time."
Judges 4:4 (ESV)

Isaiah

There was also Isaiah who wrote many chapters of the bible and gave us much revelation.

Isaiah's Wife

"And I went to the prophetess, and she conceived and bore a son..."
Isaiah 8:3 (ESV)

Hosea

Hosea is another one of my favorite prophets. Despite having a small chapter, he radically listens to God to marry a prostitute as a sign. I honestly think most people wouldn't make that sacrifice for God, but more than that, he even buys his wife back after she cheats on him. This is a beautiful example of God's love for us.

Jeremiah

Jeremiah was a young, insecure and depressed prophet who questioned if he should stay in the ministry. This insecure prophet changed the course of history with his accurate prophecies to leaders and people.

Elijah

Elijah was a powerful prophet who called down fire from heaven, killed a bunch of false prophets, and did miracles.

Miriam the dancing Prophet

"Then Miriam the prophet,
Aaron's sister, took a timbrel in her hand,
and all the women followed her,
with timbrels and dancing."

Exodus 15:20 (NIV)

I love Miriam because unlike Deborah, she is a light-hearted prophetess; she was leading the women in dance and song, while Deborah was directing men into war. These differences are allowed in God's people. "Soft" and "Lioness" women can both speak for Him.

Elisha

I thought Elisha was worth noting because his mantle was so heavy that it was double the size of Elijah's, and Elijah did miracles. He was also mentored by Elijah, which is a great biblical example of how prophets can be mentored if possible. So when he received the mantle, he was ready, at least to some extent. He had a thicker mantle then Elijah, so some training would still ensue.

Joel

Joel prophesied about Pentecost way before it happened.

David

Did you know David was actually a prophet?

*"Brothers, I can tell you with confidence that the patriarch David died and was buried, and his tomb is with us to this day. **But he was a prophet** and knew that God had promised him on oath that He would place one of his descendants on his throne."*
Acts 2:29-30(BSB)

Yes, we often know him as a worshipper, a man after God's own heart or a king, but David was also a prophet. A king that was a prophet. I like that. But David wasn't a perfect king; he slept with a married man's wife and had the man killed. But he repented and kept his position, even though he sadly lost his son over this. We all fall short, even prophets; even *king* prophets. Did you know that being a prophet doesn't have to mean in the church only? David was a king over all the people of Israel, yet he was prophet. Don't put God in a box. With different prophets He does different things.

There are many more but,

As you can see there are both old and new testament prophets and prophetesses; both men and women.

**God has always used prophets to
speak to His people, and He still does.**

**You don't need a worldly ordination
to be a prophet.**

Kay Story: I want to tell you a story about how anyone can prophesy. One day my mom decided to take a homeless woman home from church. On the way home, we were talking about the prophetic. I prophesied over her and she was shocked. She asked me how I did it, and I told her that she could do it too. I taught her an abridged version of this book in the back seat of my mom's car on the way home. I told her she could practice on me, so she did. She was shocked that she was seeing visions right there in the back of the car. This woman had no job and was living in a women's homeless shelter when they could fit her in, and yet she was able to tap into God's Spirit and share a word of the Lord with me. I hope you don't disqualify yourself because of status or where you are at in life. God can and will speak to you if you seek Him.

I hear people sometimes thinking that you are only allowed to speak as a prophet if you get a specific certification from a ministry. Let me be clear, this has got to be the most ridiculous thing

I have ever heard! A worldly piece of paper by a man cannot make you a prophet. No! Our ordination as prophets comes from before our birth and from God alone! We see this in the book of Jeremiah; Jeremiah is ordained by the Lord before he was even born!

"Before I formed you in the womb I knew you, before you were born I set you apart; I appointed you as a prophet to the nations."
Jeremiah 1:5 (NIV)

Whew! Sorry, I get so fired up here as I just cringe thinking about people thinking that a paper qualifies someone to be a prophet. It is simply not true. Now that being said, I think that getting education on prophecy is good so that you don't make a ton of mistakes. But God chooses you and makes you a prophet. Schools are more like bumpers when you go bowling. They keep you in the lane when you are first starting, but eventually the bumpers aren't necessary as you know the flow of the Holy Ghost.

AM I A PROPHET?

People are always wondering whether or not they are prophets, and everyone around them is also wondering the same. So how do you know if you or someone else is? You need to ask God! Let's pause for a second and ask God shall we? Take a second and ask God:

"Lord, am I a prophet?"

For you see, the title of Prophet does not come by achievement of a certain amount of correct prophetic words, or by a church agreeing that you are a prophet. Rather, it is a position ordained by God. So let some stress off your shoulders; you don't have to try to become a prophet, it is something God decides. Now, whether you are a good prophet or not is another story.

Here are some characteristics of a typical prophet, although not all prophets are the same:

- They usually have a hard time doing anything besides what the Lord is telling them.

- They have a deep care for people knowing God for real and not just as head knowledge.

- They are sensitive people most of the time, and they notice the slightest thing.

- They care a lot about obedience to God.

One of the downsides to being very sensitive is you can get offended very easily, so it is important to guard your heart from being offended as a prophet. Trust me, I have experienced this; my heart notices the slightest jab and I have to be careful not to become offended. Jesus knew all the thoughts of man, and as you tap more into your prophetic anointing you will know people's thoughts. Don't freak out, remember that you have the mind of Christ. But sometimes when you see that people have evil thoughts toward you it is easy to get offended. I have not always done the best at this and am still learning to forgive more.

If you are a prophet/prophetess or one that speaks for God and you want to do a good job at it, you need to have a life of continued sanctification. Why does this matter? Because you have to understand; the more sin and lies in our heart, the harder it is to hear God. And the harder it is to hear God, the more likely it is that you will either stop delivering words (and therefore have a very small prophetic ministry), or you will deliver many words but they will be inaccurate.

Though no prophet is sinless, as we see David and Abraham where both prophets that sinned; we must strive to live holy before the Lord. One way to keep up with this is simply asking the Lord to reveal anything in your heart that He wants to change. Do this on a regular basis. You can do it daily or throughout the day. This is different than condemnation. The devil may try to condemn you, telling you your sins over and over again and offering no peace, but the Lord will convict you, asking you to change. Remember, the bible says that the Lord disciplines those that He loves (Proverbs 3:12, Hebrews 12:6). We should be a people who are continually trying to eliminate sin out of our lives.

We must come to a point as Christians and Prophets where we go from sin confession to sin eradication.

One way we can do this is accountability. When I was overcoming a certain sin in my life I had an accountability group in order to get clean. You may need to do something similar if it is something you cannot easily change. This is one of the best things I ever did in my life. I know it might not seem like a big deal, but the bible says when there are two, one can help the other when they fall. (Ecclesiastes 4:10) There is also something about being fully known and not judged.

I gotta say, if you are in an accountability group where you are being judged, try talking to them about it, and if they continue to be judgmental, find a new group. You may not be able to open with everyone as the bible tells us to guard our heart above all things. If you fall confess it to a safe group, and allow them to pray for you and help you evaluate what to do next.

Always evaluate what happened if you are struggling with a certain sin. Try journaling out your feelings. This has helped me immensely. Being able to release all your feelings to God will help get all the junk out of your heart and head so you can just hear Him.

I overcame the sin I was dealing with because of many factors, but one was identifying how I got into the situation in the first place. Think about your mindset. Why did I think that? How did I get there? Was it watching a bad movie, having a bad conversation, was I tired and wasn't thinking? Evaluate and figure out what happened, so the same sin doesn't keep happening again. Often times we are people of patterns and predictable behavior, and we may not understand we are like this until we stop and evaluate. As you journal and think, you will start to notice patterns and this will help you correct your behavior. You must remember that one of the fruits of the spirit is self-control. If you cannot control your behavior, you need to figure out why. This is not a thing of God and needs to be revealed. The truth sets free, be honest with yourself. Even if you are embarrassed to tell others, tell God.

One of the other ways we need to be sanctified as prophets, or prophetic people, is to stay humble. Don't think you are better than those who do not understand spiritual things. You are not. The only reason you understand is because Jesus revealed them to you. I often see this in churches that focus only on the prophetic or supernatural healing. We can become puffed up and think we are better than those "less spiritual" people. I and many of my fellow colleagues in ministry school did this, so much so that our Prophetic Director came in and made us all repent of it. We all cried as we realized we had become arrogant, thinking we were better than others who could not prophesy or did not believe these things. Pride (Leviathan) is a sneaky demon that can make your heart very far from love. Remember, love is the most important thing and all prophetic words should flow out of love, as we are supposed to *"Pursue love, and earnestly desire the spiritual gifts, especially that you may prophesy"* (1 Corinthians 14:1, ESV). But the way we get to prophecy is supposed to be out of love. Out of our love for people we prophesy to help them and direct them in what God has for them by giving them His words.

Start praying for people if you want to get words for them. I do this before I do a conference. I print out a list of the names and just start praying over them. Anything I feel in the spirit I just pray over them. There is no need to know a person in the flesh. The spirit can reveal all things. If you are not holding your own meetings, you can begin by praying for your small group at church, your church as a whole, your friends, your family, a certain city, etc. As you are praying over these people, see if God will say anything to you about them. You may see a vision or hear a word or a scripture verse may come to your heart. You can also just read scripture while you are praying and the Lord may highlight a verse for the person to share.

Then that which you do in secret, do in the light if the Lord leads you. Pray for them and see if you start to see a vision or feel a prompting, and then share. If you are not sure if it is God, just say that. You can say "I think I may be feeling something from the Lord for you, may I share?" Most people will say yes.

Prophecy is birthed out of caring for people.

If God told you that you were not a prophet in the previous exercise, do not think "Well, I should stop reading this". Every believer has access to the prophetic, even if they aren't a prophet. Developing your prophetic gift is important, as we are told to lust after prophecy. It doesn't say only prophets should do this, but all God's children should be trained in prophecy. Why? Because it helps other people and can be exactly what they need. Prophecy helps people and we are all helpers.

If you are a pastor, apostle or other kind of leader you may need to train others in this or deliver a prophetic word to your people weekly. It doesn't mean you are necessarily a prophet, but you can still use this gift to help your people no matter your title. Which leads me into the next question.

CAN OTHER OFFICES PROPHESY?

Yes! All God's people are called to prophesy! The bible tells us to prophesy! It doesn't specify that only prophets should prophesy.

> *"Pursue love, and earnestly desire the spiritual gifts, especially that you may prophesy."*
> *1 Corinthians 14:1 (ESV)*

For the prophet, this is their primary job. They are constantly getting messages for others. The reason the Lord says "especially" about prophecy over other spiritual gifts is because it allows the Lord to speak to people, and the Lord is all about speaking to His children and to those He is wooing that way. But even if you are not a prophet, you can still encourage. You don't have to be in the fivefold either. You can be a custodian at a small grocery store and the Lord can come upon you with a word to share to a shopper at the store. Do not disqualify yourself. In fact, this is similar to how I started. My ministry existed before there was a title. I prophesied over people in bathrooms, in parking lots, at houses, in cars… anywhere. Though I did serve in church, I was mainly called outside the church in that season.

Eventually however, the Lord switched me to serve primarily inside the church to train the body in what I learned. At one time I even led a small group out to the streets to share God's love prophetically and minister healing to people outside the four walls of church. But then He moved me inside to deal with the saints. You can be a church prophet or a street prophet. One is not better than the other, they are just different. And the seasons can always change. Allow the Lord to use you wherever He desires.

Kay Story: True story, one time before my ministry started I was attending a conference in south Florida. As I was stepping out to use the restroom, I had a thought; "I wonder if God could use me in the bathroom?" When I got there, I saw a girl and her friend outside the bathroom and she was praying for her. I thought this was interesting and felt "Okay Lord, yes you can use me in the bathroom." So I went to the bathroom, and when I came back out and they were still there. I had never met these people, but they asked me to pray for her. I wasn't sure why they would ask me, as I wasn't working or speaking at the conference. These people didn't know me. But the anointing they knew and they knew if I prayed for her something would happen. So I prophesied and prayed over the woman, and her friend said "prophesy over me too!" So I did, and then someone else came and then they brought their family and a whole line began to form, so much so that the ministry workers gave us a small room for me to prophesy over people. Why am I sharing this with you right now? Because the anointing will open doors anywhere He pleases and no man can shut them! You can be used anywhere, even the bathroom. Be ready in season and out of season as the Lord can use you anywhere.

I want you to consider this: The faucet is always on. His Spirit is always inside you, so it is always flowing. He never grows tired or weary and can always speak. You just need to keep yourself in order, so He can always use you.

CHARACTER IN PROPHETS

Now let's talk about the inside of a prophet: the character. I want you to get this:

Just because someone is a prophet doesn't mean they have good or bad character.

Check out these examples:

Good Prophets can be called "Messengers", an office Jesus says is more than a prophet. Check out what Jesus says about John the Baptist:

"Then what did you go out to see? A prophet? Yes, I tell you, and ***more than a prophet.*** *This is the one about whom it is written: 'I will send my* ***messenger*** *ahead of you, who will prepare your way before you.'"*
Matthew 11:9-10 (NIV)
(Jesus referring to John the Baptist)

I believe this probably related to the fact that Jesus believed that John was one of the greatest men to have ever lived.

"I tell you the truth, of all who have ever lived, none is greater than John the Baptist."
Matthew 11:11 (NLT)

If you are a righteous prophet there is no telling what honor the Lord will bestow on you. So become a good prophet or prophetess. Work on your character and obedience.

However, as we know, not all prophets are like John the Baptist... some are Jonahs.

"Jonahs" are stubborn prophets. It is not that they don't hear God, it is that they don't listen or fight God on everything. Jonah was like this as we see below:

"Now the word of the Lord came to Jonah the son of Amittai, saying, 'Arise, go to Nineveh, that great city, and cry out against it; for their wickedness has come up before Me.' But Jonah arose to flee to Tarshish from the presence of the Lord. He went down to Joppa, and found a ship going to Tarshish; so he paid the fare, and went down into it, to go with them to Tarshish from the presence of the Lord."
Jonah 1:1-3 (NKJV)

Jonah would not deliver the word that the Lord had called him to deliver. He was rebellious to the Lord... but he was still a prophet of the

Lord. You can be a prophet and still be rebellious to the Lord. That doesn't mean it's ok to be rebellious, but the bible doesn't say Jonah was a false prophet because he was disobedient. In fact, it says he was a prophet. Many of us can relate as we have all been stubborn from time to time. But we all need to learn to be less stubborn if and when God speaks, so we don't end up in a big fish for days. Jonah did eventually repent, and went and delivered the word he was supposed to. It is never too late to turn from a Jonah to a John.

I know it can be hard sometimes, as often what God tells you to do goes against the world or what you may want or what you think is "right" in your own eyes. But, you must still listen. You could be a Noah and save the human race from extinction just because of your obedience. You could be like Deborah and give a word to a military officer that helped free the Israelites. Listen, I know it is hard sometimes, and if we're honest we have all not listened to God at some point. But forgive yourself, and start every day fresh. His mercies are new each morning.

"The steadfast love of the Lord never ceases; his mercies never come to an end; they are

new every morning; great is your faithfulness."
Lamentations 3:22-23 (ESV)

DON'T BE A BAD FINANCIAL PROPHET

We have all seen a lot of abuse of finances in the prophetic; "Give $1,000 and we will pray/ prophesy over you." I saw this in a church once and I was stunned. I was shocked that they would ask for money to pray for people, and that people would actually pay so much money to be prayed over or prophesied over by this man. But they did.

Don't ever charge for prophecy. Charging for a conference/meeting to pay for a building rental is different than saying, "Give me $5 and I will give you a word from God." I honestly don't even like having to charge for meetings, but paying for things like a building, flights for speakers and conference supplies adds up. Some ministries are at a point where they have the funds to foot the bill, and we have had free meetings before when the Lord has told us to, but this is very different then charging for prayer and prophecy.

Being in ministry can be hard when you are strapped for cash or donations are down. You might try to make people pay you, but I would encourage you to instead go into prayer and ask God for the money. He will either manifest it or He will put you to work. In the bible, Paul made tents and received donations

"Paul went to visit them, and he stayed and worked with them because they were tentmakers by trade, just as he was."
Acts 18:2-3 (BSB)

Even so, you have done well to share with me in my present difficulty. As you know, you Philippians were the only ones who gave me financial help when I first brought you the Good News and then traveled on from Macedonia. No other church did this.
Philippians 4:14-15 (NLT)

This dual ability allowed him to not walk in drought. If nothing was coming in, he could always work. Early on in our ministry I would hand make pillows. It was kind of ridiculous at first because I was sowing them by hand and it would take me 2-3 weeks to deliver the product, but then my husband bought me a sowing machine and I was able to make a couple hundred dollars a month sowing pillows. This helped when donations weren't high or in between meetings.

Find a tent or pillow-like activity for when your ministry needs cash. People don't often understand the cost of doing ministry. Website fees, credit card fees, traveling fees, building rentals, air time fees, etc. Ask the Lord how these bills are going to get paid rather than going into a ton of debt.

Over time, the pillow making died down and I focused more on book creation. But I will always be thankful for the pillows. They helped Ryan and I eat many times in those early years.

I hope this chapter helped you know that you can prophesy. But now that you know that you can, let's talk about how.

CHAPTER 3

HOW TO GET
A WORD
FROM GOD

I want to talk to you now about how you may receive a prophetic word from the Lord. We need to understand this truth in a community of prophetic people:

Prophets have different ways of getting words, but some biblical truths stay the same.

Here are some of the ways prophets hear God:

- Through dreams.

- The Holy Spirit whispers something inside them.

- The Holy Spirit highlights something outside of them (it could be something in nature, a color, etc.).

- God audibly speaks.

This is all fine as long as it is of the right spirit. We should be more concerned about the spirit behind a revelation rather than how the revelation is received. Some people go on and on about how they got this revelation and people are amazed at the story. But what really matters more is whether or not they are hearing the right spirit, *not* how cool the story is displayed.

There are essentially two types of prophetic reception:

Received without Intention: This is when you are not trying to get a word form the Lord, but it just happens. You could be just walking through the grocery store and God drops something in your spirit. This cannot be controlled as God is not respecter of persons, so if He wants to talk to you He will. This can come in different ways whether sleeping or just abruptly like a burning bush.

"...God is no respecter of persons"
Acts 10:34 (KJV)
(Also see Romans 2:11)

Received with Intention: This is when you are trying to get a prophetic word from God for yourself, someone else or some thing (i.e. Church, business, nation, etc.). This is more of what we will be talking about in this book, as the former you cannot control. Though we cannot make God speak, as He does what He wishes, you can develop a relationship with Him that is so intimate that you can almost always get a word for someone.

Kay's Wisdom: I want to tell you about something you can have access to: a faucet that does not turn off. There is a place in the prophetic where you can always get a word, unless the Lord wants you to rest. You must be trustworthy before the Lord in order to receive this. My gift allows me to prophesy over almost every single person in the room at all times, though I do not always do that because there is a fatigue that sometimes comes afterwards. People do not always understand this, but there really can be a fatigue that comes afterward; you may feel very hungry or stay in bed for hours or even days. After I put on a conference where I pour out a lot, I am often tired and need to refuel. If God grants you this gift, allow yourself space to fill back up after pouring out. Spend time with Him, sleep, eat, do things you enjoy... take care of yourself. This gift has a cost.

Remember this wisdom: If you can get a prophetic word for 1 person, you can get a word for 10 people. If you can get words for 10 people, you can get 20 words. Just listen and repeat. Many people get excited after they give one accurate word, and they just walk around happy about this, but there is more. You can give words to everyone in the whole room, and when you do, you can begin to change an area. When the whole room sees that all their secrets were revealed by God, they start following God with a new fire, knowing the realness of God in a deeper way.

Why does this happen? Because the Bible says that Jesus knew all the thoughts of man, and as you tap into the mind of Christ, you will know all the thoughts of man as well. Be a good steward of this, not exposing people's secrets in unloving ways but rather seeking God's wisdom for their life and encouraging them in the right way. Sometimes you are not supposed to share with them what the Lord showed you. It is just for you to know for their protection or prayer. Use wisdom. There is more than you think.

That being said. Let me show you how to get a word. The first thing you need to do is:

SEEK GOD

"You will seek me and find me when you seek me with all your heart."
Jeremiah 29:13 (NIV)

When trying to get a "word", we must remember that it is God who gives the words. So we must first seek Him in order to receive a prophetic word for others or ourselves. Start making yourself long for God in your heart and thought life, then desire to seek His face and know His voice. You may start to see a vision or hear something.

Kay Tip: Developing a lifestyle of seeking God helps. Asking God about everything will help you in your accuracy of hearing Him. People that only seek God every once in a while don't necessarily hear Him as well, for they are not as tuned in to the sound of His voice as often. When you develop a lifestyle of seeking Him about all things, you will hear Him better. I even ask Him where to go out to eat or what to buy. When writing an email, I may ask Him what to say or if He has anything to change in the email. People may call this spiritually legalistic, but I call this life. Coming to a point where you trust His choices over yours is hard, but it is life. For He knows things you don't know and can protect or propel you.

An Exercise to Try: Spend a whole day asking God about everything. Ask Him when to eat, what to eat, when to go to sleep, when to wake up, when to go shopping, when to make a call, what to say on the call. As you do this, your accuracy will increase. If it seems chaotic the first day, try again the next day. I have chosen to live my life like this, as I have decided I only want to do what my Lord wants me to do, nothing less. He is my father and I trust Him more than I could ever trust me. I have laid down my life for Him. You may not feel the same way and I do not judge you for it. But the more you practice daily surrender, the more God will reveal His secrets to you. Things will also make more sense in your life and you will have more breakthroughs.

You may wonder how I can do this all time. I made a commitment many years ago to be a servant for God. As I have been his servant, I have become a friend and a daughter. But even though I have the right not to live this way, I choose to, for I trust Him more than anything or anyone, even myself. I put no confidence in me to come up with ideas. His ideas are mine now. Choose if you will to live this way. The choice is yours. But regardless, living surrendered for a day or two will help you understand the movement of his Spirit. This is what many call practicing His Presence. You start to notice when He tells you to do something, and if you listen and do it, a certain peace will come, versus when you disobey you feel a certain restlessness in your soul. This restlessness is mourning the Holy Spirit.

Pay attention to peace, but also be on guard for a false peace that seems like God but does not respond "Yes Jesus Christ has come in the flesh" when discerning the spirits. This is often python pretending. Discern the spirits and have peace.

By letting Him lead you in all things, when you go to prophesy you will do the same thing as this surrendered routine. Simply listen and do. You will feel His peace on certain words and not others. Use this peace to ensure you're using the right phrasing when you prophesy.

We can make things too complicated. Do not over question. I know this can be hard, but things will not always make natural sense in the prophetic. You must understand this to move ahead. If you never see any fruit to anything you have done that you felt was God, there may be a problem. But if you have continuous fruit keep along the journey.

It is often the little things that take us to where we need to go with Jesus, one day at a time. It will seem awkward at first, asking about everything, but you will find His ways are the best ways. In time it will all make sense.

Let's jump back into the teaching:

WAIT

"Wait for the Lord; be strong and take heart and wait for the Lord."
Psalm 27:14 (NIV)

I love how this verse above says, "Wait for the Lord" twice in the same sentence. You want to wait until you see a vision or sense His voice; you don't want to make something up. Otherwise it is an imagination and not a vision, and we are called to cast imaginations down.

"Casting down imaginations, and every high thing that exalteth itself against the knowledge of God, and bringing into captivity every thought to the obedience of Christ"
2 Corinthians 10:5 (KJV)

You may have to wait a long time in the beginning as you are learning which voice is which, but over time it will come more quickly, like a flow. Be patient. God's voice is worth it. I had a girl who once was very discouraged that she couldn't hear God very well. She felt like out of the girls in our community, she heard God the least. But she stuck with it and became extremely sensitive to the Lord. I have seen this happen with several girls. Stay in the wait if you are not hearing anything yet.

Just because something is fuzzy doesn't mean it is not from God. We prophesy in part and know in part.

> *"For we know in part, and we prophesy in part."*
> *1 Corinthians 13:9 (KJV)*

Sometimes you are not getting the whole picture and are just called to deliver part of the message. That is okay. If someone wants you to explain something but you don't have an explanation, don't make one up. Just say, "I am not sure, maybe in your prayer time God will reveal more to you."

Kay Note: Let me be honest with you. Most of the visions I get from God are rather fuzzy or not extremely vivid, and yet at a conference or meeting I am expected to and do deliver the word instantly. It is not some clear, long, epic vision. It is a small vision; a small trail, if you will, that I follow. The trail of breadcrumbs, left by the Holy Spirit. Just follow it. It takes faith to follow it, but just trust and go. If you doubt, you will start to lose the vision.

"But let him ask in faith, with no doubting, for he who doubts is like a wave of the sea driven and tossed by the wind."
James 1:6 (NKJV)

Once you have tested the spirits, believe and go. Oh, it can take you to some beautiful places. Check out this simple story:

Kay Story: One time I was praying over a woman, and all I saw was a vision of coffee beans spilling on the ground. God didn't tell me anything specific to say, so I just told her, "I see coffee beans spilling on the ground." I didn't see her after that for a couple weeks, and then one day she told me that the vision I had shared with her meant a lot to her. She told me she was addicted to coffee and God was telling her to get rid of the coffee in her life. It was a simple vision, but it impacted this woman. Just say what is said to you no more. Had I made something up, I could have hurt her. She knew what it meant. God protected her by not telling me the fullness of her issue, but just enough so that she knew what she needed to do.

LET IT FLOW

Let the flow be spontaneous, don't try to control it. Just say and do as the Spirit is guiding you. When we try to control the Spirit, we are walking against the Spirit because,

> *"...where the Spirit of the Lord is,*
> *there is freedom."*
> *2 Corinthians 3:17 (NIV)*

Let the Lord be free to move through you, and the results will be amazing. In other words, don't try to control what you hear. Just listen and repeat. I want to encourage you to just speak what He says to the person. Do not add your own words. For a vision may not mean anything to you, but it might mean something to them.

Obviously as I said before, make sure you are hearing the right spirit by asking if Jesus Christ has come in the flesh. There are false Jesus spirits roaming around these days, and we want to make sure it is the real Jesus. So how do we know it is from God, besides the common "if it's love it is God" thoughts about prophecy?

Learn how to test the spirits as the bible tells us to:

*"Beloved, **believe not every spirit, but try the spirits whether they are of God:** because many false prophets are gone out into the world. **Hereby know ye the Spirit of God: Every spirit that confesseth that Jesus Christ is come in the flesh is of God: And every spirit that confesseth not that Jesus Christ is come in the flesh is not of God: and this is that spirit of antichrist,** whereof ye have heard that it should come; and even now already is it in the world."*
1 John 4:1-3 (KJV)

As you can see from this scripture, the bible clearly tells us that we should test the spirits. It also tells us how. It says the way we know which spirit is from Jesus is by what the spirit confesses. The spirits that confess that Jesus Christ has come in the flesh are of God, and the spirits that do not are of the antichrist. So how do we practically figure out if a spirit confesses that Jesus Christ has come in the flesh? Well quite simply, ask it! If you hear a "voice" talking to you while walking around or in the prayer closet, you need to ask it, "Has Jesus Christ come in the flesh?" Then wait to see what it says. It may respond "Yes, Jesus Christ has come in the flesh" or it may respond "No he's hasn't". Once you get a "Yes, Jesus Christ has come in the flesh" response, listen intently because the Lord is speaking to you. If it is a negative response of "No, Jesus Christ has not come in the flesh!" then a demon is talking to you, and you need to rebuke that thing! Don't freak out though; remember that you have ALL authority!

"Behold, I have given you authority to tread on serpents and scorpions, and over all the power of the enemy, and nothing shall hurt you."
Luke 10:19 (ESV)

Once you are hearing the correct spirit and know Jesus, Yahweh, an Angel, or the Holy Spirit are speaking to you, then just listen. Let the Lord show you a vision, say something, lead you to a scripture verse or highlight an item. This may sound weird, but some of you know this to be true. Sometimes the Lord will say nothing, but just highlight something. You may feel His presence on an item, word, location, etc. If you feel this, ask Him more questions. Don't assume, just listen.

Warning: Do not get lost in signs or think certain things always mean the same thing. Allow the Lord to tell you fresh revelation as He wills. Some people are addicted to numerology, and I am not against studying what numbers mean in the bible, but this cannot become an idol where every number always means something. This obsessive thinking process can actually be rather demonic and has trapped some of God's believers into systems instead of relationship. Be open to the Lord telling you that anything means anything. In the bible there are different dreams about bread, and in these dreams bread means different things. Why? Because the Spirit is not a formula. Although you and Jesus can develop you own language together, where certain things mean something specific to you, even this cannot become a formula. Let go of the formula and live in the flow.

CHAPTER 4

HOW AND WEHN TO DELIVER A WORD

WHEN TO GIVE A WORD

When you feel confident you got a word from the Lord, now what? A good question to ask the Lord is "When do you want me to give this person the word?" One time the Lord made me hang onto a word for someone for a whole year! It was killing me, but I did it. Why? Because the Lord was testing my faithfulness to Him, but also the person couldn't have received that word too soon, or they would have tried to do it in their own strength.

Now there *are* times to give a word right away of course, but thinking this is all the time is wrong. I often see people young in the prophetic interrupting everyone to tell them they have a word. But sometimes this is rude, and they are actually just trying to bring attention to themselves, even if it is unknowingly. One of the fruits of the spirit is self-control, and if you cannot "control" when you give a word, it might be a compulsion in your heart. Pause and wait. If He says to, then of course do it, but just ask and you will have more fruit. A word given in the right season will bear more fruit then one out of season.

It is good to wait on the Lord to give a word. I know it can be hard, as you are so excited that the Lord would speak that you just want to share. But wait on his timing beloved. In due season a harvest is waiting for you or for them.

HOW TO GIVE A WORD

Now that you know what the word is and when to give the word, the next question is "*How should I give the word?*" This can mean many things, but **Tone** and **Mode of Communication** are probably the two most relevant aspects. For example, should it be a stern tone you use when you say it? Should it be a causal tone? Should it be asked like a question? Asking these kinds of questions about the word will really help emotionally care for the person on the receiving end, as you do not know the best way for them to receive the word, but God does.

Another thing to consider is how you will get it to them. Will it be in a note? In person? On the phone? Through e-mail? This may seem meticulous, but God cares about the details. It will honestly take you one minute to ask Him when, how, and which mode of communication, and this creates the exact way God wants the person's heart to be cared for. Remember, *"God is Love."* (1 John 4:8, ESV), and giving special attention to the way a person would receive a word is the most loving thing you can do. So take an extra minute and ask for the person's sake and for yours!

Another thing worth noting is that you may need to do a prophetic act as opposed to actually saying something to show the person what God is saying. This is not all the time, but it does happen once in a while. So be open to the Holy Spirit telling you to do that as well.

If a person does not receive a word, it's possible that they will get mad or even yell at you. You may not want to deal with that, but the truth is, sometimes some people will not receive a word, even when it *is* from God. Don't be afraid though if someone yells at you, people did the same thing to the prophets that have gone before you! If you do even a small study on the prophets in the bible you will see them being rejected. But don't go looking for rejection either. Walk in love and consideration, and you will have less drama. Jeremiah wanted to quit his ministry after he was struck by someone in the church house after speaking a word of the Lord.

"Whenever I speak, I cry out proclaiming violence and destruction. So the word of the Lord has brought me insult and reproach all day long. But if I say, "I will not mention his word or speak anymore in his name," his word is in my heart like a fire, a fire shut up in my bones. I am weary of holding it in; indeed, I cannot."
Jeremiah 20:8-9 (NIV)

Earlier in the chapter, a chief governor of the house of the Lord strikes Jeremiah when he speaks. He even puts him in the stocks before eventually letting him go free. But Jeremiah couldn't give up. When the Lord is in you like a burning fire it is hard to not speak for Him.

It can be hard when someone tells you they do not accept the word, yells at you, or is just mean or rude. But you have to remind yourself that they are not rejecting you, they are rejecting God. What is going on inside them is between them and God, as the word is from God, not you. Don't take it personally. I've had to learn to have firmer skin being in this ministry. But it is not all bad. You will change people's lives with this gift. People will go from being confused to knowing what they are supposed to do, they will be healed of diseases, they will have vision for their future. They can even have their heart healed from a prophetic word. The prophetic is a beautiful thing. Don't give up on the prophetic; the very testimony of Jesus, just because someone has issues with God.

Some will prophesy small things and some will prophesy large things. Some prophecies will be one word and some will be a whole paragraph. Don't be impressed by one or the other. A word is word. Sometimes God wants to say one thing, and sometimes another. Different prophets have different relationships with God, and so their words may come out differently. They also have differing levels of faith. Check this verse out:

"We have different gifts, according to the grace given to each of us. If your gift is prophesying, then prophesy in accordance with your faith; if it is serving, then serve; if it is teaching, then teach"
Romans 12:6-7 (NIV)

This gift says to prophesy according to your faith. This seems weird, but faith and prophecy are intertwined. You must have faith to prophesy that someone is going to get healed of something. You must have faith to believe they are going to pay off their house. Without faith, prophecy can turn into reporting. The world does plenty of that; just saying what is happening. But with Jesus, and His power in us and through us, we can change what will happen. God has good gifts for His children, and part of prophecy is delivering those gifts in the Spirit as a prophetic message.

CHAPTER 5

WHY WE
GET IT WRONG
SOMETIMES

I think there are 5 main reasons we sometimes miss it in the prophetic:

1. **Wounded Hearts**
2. **Demonic Voices**
3. **Idols**
4. **Distractions**
5. **Wrong Biblical Teaching**

WOUNDED HEARTS

One of the main reasons I see people miss the voice of God is that their heart is broken/ wounded. Here is an example:

Say that you were abused as a child by your father. You may have a filter that says "God is mean" because your father was mean. So when you prophesy over another person, you prophesy with the filter that God is mean, and your tone and some of the words are wrong. This is just one of countless possibilities of filters people have developed that gives them false words, even if they may have a good motive. They may genuinely want to deliver a word from the Lord, but their broken heart makes it come out wrong. Our heart and the Holy Spirit are both inside of us, and when our heart is wounded in a certain way, it makes it loud and not peaceful when trying to hear from God. This loudness makes it harder to hear the Holy Spirit, and so we think the sound we hear is the Lord when in fact it is our own heart.

Ask the Lord right now if there are any filters in your heart that have caused you to prophesy over other people incorrectly. Ask Him to heal them or remove them and go through the heart healing process.

If we are not intentional about continually allowing the Lord to heal our heart, it can cause serious problems in prophesying. But thankfully one of the reasons Jesus came was so we would have access to heart healing. In Luke 4 Jesus says:

> *"he hath sent me to heal the*
> *brokenhearted..."*
> *Luke 4:18 (KJV)*

Note: Some versions of the bible including the NIV omit this part of Luke 4, however the KJV, RSV and NKJV all have this verse in there.

How Heart Healing Works

Basically, the point of heart healing is to redeem or bring peace to certain moments in your life where you were wounded or developed wrong thinking. You start by allowing the Lord to show you a moment He would like to redeem. After this, you may ask Him where He was in the moment and allow Him to show you. In traumatic moments we can often feel like God wasn't there, and this can ruin our thoughts about God. These thoughts and feelings need to be healed. You can also ask Him what lies you believe about the situation and let Him speak the truth to you. Then you need to meditate on that truth until you fully believe it. You can also ask Him if there are any demonic strongholds from your past, as demons could have come in through a certain event and are rooted because of something that happened.

Note: If you were (or someone was) the victim of abuse, a demonic spirit can enter into you (or the victim) through a soul tie with the abuser. This is not the victim's fault; the tie just needs to be broken off through prayer, and in more extreme cases, fasting.

Here is an example of when someone may need heart healing. Say a girl is raped by a father figure in her life, so she thinks God is sexual towards her. This causes her to prophesy in a way that has hints of sexuality in it. In heart healing, she would need to allow Jesus into the moment she was raped and ask Him what He would like to say to her about it. If done correctly, the hint of sexuality in her prophecies should be removed.

Objection to Heart Healing

Some people believe looking back into the past is not biblical because of this verse:

"But his wife (Lot's wife) looked back from behind him, and she became a pillar of salt." *(Genesis 19:26)*

However, in the very next verse Abraham looks back at the same destruction and is not punished or turned into salt! That was a command specifically for Lot and his wife.

"And Abraham went early in the morning to the place he had stood before the Lord. Then he looked toward Sodom and

Gomorrah, and toward all the land of the plain; and he saw, and behold, the smoke of the land which went up like the smoke of a furnace. And it came to pass, when God destroyed the cities of the plain, that God remembered Abraham..."
Genesis 19:27-29 (NKJV)

Not returning to the past is not a command for everyone all the time! We must allow God to redeem our past, if He wills, through returning to moments to heal false mindsets or demonic strongholds.

Jesus came for your whole life to be restored, and every area that the enemy stole in the past! God can redeem moments and restore your heart if you let Him into your heart long enough! Isn't that great news? Take time right now and ask the Lord if there are any memories you want to heal that may make you prophesy over people incorrectly.

Also, don't think this is a one-time thing. You may be healed from certain seasons, but then you may get new wounds and need new healings. Have "heart checkups" with the Lord as necessary.

DEMONIC VOICES

Another reason people miss it when prophesying is that the voice they are hearing was never God to begin with. Obviously this is pretty self-explanatory, but I will address it a little bit so we all understand. It is possible to go into the prayer closet or be in a meeting and genuinely try to hear God, but a demon pretending to be God deceives you. Make sure you discern the spirits as we talked about earlier, as the enemy can pretend to be Jesus, God, or say he is an angel. Yes this is scary, but it is true. If you deny this truth, you will miss it when prophesying. Know that there are false Jesus spirits, and be on guard by testing the spirits. For a more in-depth study on this, see my book *Discerning The Spirits: The Next Revival.*

**Every time we engage in sin, we follow
a voice that isn't from God.**

The more you follow false spirits, the harder it is going to be to hear God. This is because these spirits are loud, and as you follow them (sin), you develop a stronghold and it gets harder to hear God.

IDOLS

Another reason people miss it when prophesying is having idols. I had a girl come to me many years ago distraught about a "word" some other girl had given her. The girl basically said "The Lord has told me that you are supposed to move out of the state with me and start your work there." The girl who received the word asked me if this was from God. I asked God and felt no, and that the girl simply wanted her to move with her. The girl delivering the word had an idol of loneliness, and she wanted to have a friend live where she was living with her, so she "prophesied" it to the other girl, making her confused.

This happens often, but we must not try to force our will on someone and call it prophecy. Sometimes are idols aren't necessarily bad things; this girl just was lonely and wanted a friend to move with her. It's not bad to want a friend to live with you. But it becomes bad when you call it prophesy. She should have just asked the girl to move with her rather than calling it a word of the Lord.

You can often tell an idol is present when there is no freedom for the person to make choices. Though sometimes God is firm, this is not all the time and there is often freedom for them to choose. God is a God of freedom and free will.

DISTRACTIONS

Our modern-day culture is full of distractions, and it is easy to prophesy wrong because of a distraction. Whether the distraction is your fault or not doesn't matter, you can still become inaccurate in your prophesying.

Say for example you are trying to give a word and your phone rings. This distraction can make you lose your focus on God, and make you prophesy out of what is going on with the phone or make you forget to discern the spirits and prophesy wrong. Try to learn intense focus, and do not let your mind wander when prophesying. When you're at a meeting, ignore anything else going on in the room and just listen to and follow the Holy Spirit.

WRONG BIBLICAL TEACHING
(OR THE LACK THEREOF)

Wrong (or a lack of) biblical teaching can make people prophesy wrong, because they do not know what the bible says on a matter and can just say stuff that doesn't line up with the word of God. Also, a person who does not read the word often may get less words in general because they simply have less in them to draw from.

Biblical teaching that is incorrect can taint a person's mind to think scripture means something that it does not. They may then prophesy out of an incorrect filter, and the prophesy ends up tainted. Ask the Lord to reveal to you any false things you believe about scripture so you don't prophesy incorrectly over someone. Don't become paranoid and stop prophesying, but just allow the Lord to show you things that may be off. This will increase your accuracy.

IF YOU HAVE BEEN HURT

If you have been hurt by the prophetic because the person who prophesied over you gave you a tainted prophecy, I want you know you are not alone. Even if the words were correct, but they were in the wrong tone or in the wrong timing, it can be hurtful. In some worse cases maybe the words were wrong completely and you took their advice, and it threw your life off course. Whatever has happened or will happen in the prophetic, we cannot despise prophecy. Trust me, I know. I almost gave up on prophecy myself. I almost threw it out the window. That was before I was in ministry. But I remember finding myself on the floor just crying and being like, "God, I thought this was you." But it was not Him. However, it was from that place that I learned how to hear Him well, as He taught me *how* to hear Him. From there I birthed a ministry of teaching people how to hear God and prophesy.

I want to encourage you that people's lives *will* get changed from this. There have been women and men who have cried hysterically from the words I have given to them from God, because it touched their heart so deeply. Some have laughed, some have fallen out under the anointing of God, but whatever happened, they were touched by God, and that makes it all worth it.

CHAPTER 6

WHY SOME REAL WORDS DON'T COME TO PASS

This is going to be a hard chapter to write and some of you may not be able to receive this, but I hope you do for your sake and for the sake of those around you. Sometimes real prophetic words do not come to pass because of the person they were given to. It could be due to sin related to the word, unrelated sin, or just simply unbelief or refusal of the word. I am going to try to explain this biblically as much as I can. May those that have ears let them hear.

First off, we cannot go on sinning continuously in an unrepentant way and expect all that God has prophesied over our life to happen.

"The instant I speak concerning a nation and concerning a kingdom, to pluck up, to pull down, and to destroy it, if that nation against whom I have spoken turns from its evil, I will relent of the disaster that I thought to bring upon it. And the instant I speak concerning a nation and concerning a kingdom, to build and to plant it, if it does evil in My sight so that it does not obey My voice, then I will relent concerning the good with which I said I would benefit it.
Jeremiah 18:7-10 (NKJV)

Here is an example of this in Scripture: Huldah prophesies that Josiah would have a peaceful life and be at rest for bringing his nation into repentance, but then he dies in a war. Was Huldah wrong? No. The Lord had a peaceful life of good age for him. But Josiah decided to go to war against the king of Egypt when the Lord was actually on the side of the king of Egypt. Therefore he got himself killed. He started doing evil in the sight of the Lord, and thus forfeited his promise from God.

"But as for the king of Judah, who sent you to inquire of the Lord, in this manner you shall speak to him, 'Thus says the Lord God of Israel: "Concerning the words which you have heard—because your heart was tender, and you humbled yourself before God when you heard His words against this place and against its inhabitants, and you humbled yourself before Me, and you tore your clothes and wept before Me, I also have heard you," says the Lord. "Surely I will gather you to your fathers, and you shall be gathered to your grave in peace; and your eyes shall not see all the calamity which I

will bring on this place and its inhabitants."
    2 Chronicles 34:26-28 (NKJV)

"While Josiah was king, Pharaoh Neco, king of Egypt, went to the Euphrates River to help the king of Assyria. King Josiah and his army marched out to fight him, but King Neco killed him..."
    2 Kings 23:29 (NLT)

Secondly, we must walk toward or believe the prophecy we were given. People get a prophecy that they are going to write a book, but then they refuse to pick up a pen and so the book is never written. You must walk toward your prophecy as the Lord would lead you to. This is part of the prophecy. It is like if God said, "Noah you are going to build an ark for me." But then Noah refuses to do it. There would be no ark.

Thirdly, if you refuse to believe a prophecy, it may not come to pass. If you get a prophetic word from someone and say "I refuse this" sometimes God will say "Okay" and it will not come to pass. It is not always because the prophet is wrong, it is because God listened to you.

Fourthly, it could just be unbelief in general. You felt that the word was from God when it was given, but you just have no faith that something like that could happen to you, so over time or sometimes instantly, you give up on the word. This unbelief can stop a prophecy, as you are not walking toward it in faith.

CHAPTER 7

GETTING YOUR PROPHETIC WORDS TO COME TO PASS

I couldn't tell you why words don't come to pass without telling you how to get them to come to pass.

1. Make sure it is a word from God. This seems simple but you must identify the difference between hope and a word from God. Sometimes people mistake faith for wishing. If God didn't say it, then you can't hope it into being. Ask God if He has said something. If He hasn't said it, you can still ask Him if it is okay to believe for it. Some things originate from you and that is okay, but ask God to come into agreement with it. If He says "No" or "Not yet", don't get discouraged; God knows more than you. Remember, His ways are not your ways and His thoughts are not your thoughts (Isaiah 55:8). Something might look good to you from the surface, but that doesn't mean it is actually good. Trust His yes and His no as the ultimate guide to your life. Try not to force your will on God.

2. If you can, get a scripture verse to stand on. That always helps. A prophetic word backed up by scripture is like fire. Now, what I'm talking about here is not taking a random scripture verse and trying to force a word into being. I'm talking about getting a verse to stand on that the Holy Spirit, God or Jesus has highlighted to you. We should not pull verses to try to bend them to our will. Instead, we should allow the Lord to reveal them to us. Now the verse might not say "go to Africa", but it may say "go make disciples of all nations" and maybe God highlighted that to you during prayer to confirm going to Africa. Your heart should be at peace when God highlights something. Though we can all get scared or nervous of a big word from the Lord, normally when we first realize it is Him there is peace.

Remember, God brings peace that surpasses all understanding. It is normally afterward when the devil tries to show us "how hard it will be" or how it "doesn't make sense" that we start freaking out. But the initial word should bring peace. Also remember the power of the bible; it is sharper than a double-edged sword and alive and active. When the enemy tries to tell you this cannot happen, you tell him "This is written!" Remember God's word does not return void. Print the verse out or write it down, so when you are tempted to doubt you will stand firm on it.

3. Keep the word before your eyes. Don't forget about the prophetic word you received from the Lord. This is so important. During one year of my life I had a clear goal that I wanted to get out of debt. So during that year I worked really hard and made sacrifices to be free, and I got free. But then the next year, I lost focus and didn't have super specific financial goals. Because of that I didn't really make any financial progress at all. I was devastated, but I realized that I lacked focus and lacked a clear goal. It is the same with prophetic words. What did God tell you was going to happen this year? I want to encourage you to write this in a place where you will see it constantly.

Another time, God told me a certain type of car I was going to get in prayer, and that it would come in two years. So I printed out a picture of the car from the internet, and for two years I prayed over that car, and it manifested. I did not pay a dime of my own money; it was given to me as a gift. I tell you this not to brag about a car that was manifested through prayer, but to tell you the power of keeping a vision before your eyes.

Check this verse out in 1 Timothy 1:18:

"This charge I commit unto thee, son Timothy, according to the prophecies which went before on thee, that thou by them mightest war a good warfare; holding on to faith and a good conscience..."
1 Timothy 1:18-19 (KJV)

This is such an awesome verse. Paul tells Timothy to wage war according to the prophecies that were made about him. And so should we. If you think the Devil is just going to roll over and hand you your promises on a silver platter, think again. We must wage war just like Timothy to get these things to manifest. We can do this by keeping them before our eyes, praying over them, and asking people we trust to pray over them as well. However, I will say this; I have shared my vision with people who do not come into agreement with me and it is awful. It almost tares the vision down before it even begins. So ask God who you can trust, and tell them.

4. Sow your seed! You need to be a giver if you want a word to manifest. How much you give and where you give is up to you and God. But I am telling you there is fruit for those who give seed. When I was broke I didn't have a lot of money to give, but I gave items I owned to people. Whether a necklace or a pair of earrings, you always have something to give. After you give your seed, decide what you want it to be a seed for, and keep on giving for that thing you want until it manifests. Now, you should NOT expect the harvest to manifest necessarily from the person you gave the seed to. It could come from anywhere the Lord wants to. Your job is to sow into soil that is good, and where the Lord told you to sow. God is the one that waters it.

5. Try asking God what season the prophecy is supposed to come to pass in. I often see people think something did not come to pass, but the prophecy was not for this season. Spend that extra time with God and discern when the prophecy supposed to come to pass. Remember, before God does anything He tells His servants the prophets (Amos 3:7). He may not always tell you the exact minute, but He may tell you the season or timeframe. Something like "This week" or "Next year" or "Today". If you don't hear God on specific timings yet, just wait, you will. The more time you spend with Him, and the more you clear out your heart, the more you will hear these things. Don't be afraid to ask Him. He is not scary. God is love.

> *"A man hath joy by the answer of his mouth: and a word spoken in due season, how good is it!"*
> *Proverbs 15:23 (KJV)*

6. Do your part. In our day and age I often see people that are so LAZY. They do not understand that often times they have a part to play in this.

Ask God what your role in bringing your prophetic word to pass is. If you think God is always telling you to do nothing, you may be deceived. Sometimes we do need to sit back after we have done all God asked us to do, and simply wait for Him to show up, but that's not always the case. Listen and see which season you are in so you can make sure your word manifests.

7. Do things the way He told you to do them. Don't be like Moses who struck the rock instead of speaking to it, and ended up in a wilderness. Some of you have heard my sermon on why you may be in a wilderness and how I share about how God told Moses to speak to the rock but he strikes it instead. Because of this he did not enter the promised land. He listened a little, but not fully. I know it can be easy to do things the way you want. Trust me, I know. I sometimes think "Why wouldn't we do it this way?", but God has His own reasonings and ways, and we must do our best to do things in His ways. Not ours.

8. Keep a check on your heart. In the bible it says "You have not what you ask for because the motives of your heart are to spend it on your selfish desires." (James 4:2-3). Sometimes you just want things for the wrong reasons. Yes, God says He will give you the desires of your heart, but only when they are God desires. He doesn't just give you evil desires. God is not mocked. Spend some time in the prayer closet and see *why* you want the promise. Even if it is a prophetic promise that God told you Himself, it can be delayed by wrong motives. So make sure you do a heart check in the prayer closet.

9. Spend time with Him and allow Him to adjust your sails. Let the Lord change the plans. I can't emphasize this enough. Without being open to His changes, you can easily start stepping into religious activity rather than relationship activity. Say God told you to pray at 3am every morning, but after five weeks you are really tired. You then become bitter and are angry at God for this requirement. However, maybe when you got tired you should have checked in with Him, and He may have said "Okay baby, let's move it to 4am now, as I give my beloved rest." When things seem to not be joyful or working well anymore, pause and check in. God may have switched the sails and you just need to get clued in.

CHAPTER 8

DEVELOPING CONSISTENT PRAYER TIME

If you don't get this, you won't have the results you are looking for. Without consistent prayer time, your prophetic gift will always be in and out of accuracy.

Think of talking on the telephone. If your spouse was to call you on the phone, once you heard their voice you would know it was them regardless of the number they were calling from. Why? Because you have spent enough time with them to know the sound of their voice. The more time you spend with God, the more you will know the tone of the Holy Spirit's voice. So do not lack in your time with Him. And do yourself a favor and don't spend the whole time talking. Listen. Ask questions. Ask God questions and see if He responds. And while you're doing that, think about how you know it's Him and what specifically His voice sounds like to you.

If you are in and out of the prayer closet, you can expect your gift to be in and out as well. Remember that what we do in secret is rewarded openly (Matthew 6:4-6). I have seen many times as I train up people in the prophetic, that they are unwilling to do the prayer time and so their words from God are few, or there is not a lot of power behind them. It is in the prayer closet that we learn to love people more.

In 1 Corinthians 14:1 it says to purse love and eagerly desire the spiritual gifts, specifically prophecy. But why does it say pursue love before prophecy? Because prophecy should flow out of love. Your love for people should produce prophecy. As you are praying for people, God will tell you secrets about them. If you are not praying, fewer secrets will be revealed. If you don't care about people, why would God trust you with their secrets?

How do you practically do this? Make a commitment (if the Holy Spirit allows) to pray every day for an hour or more. I honestly believe people that only spend 20 minutes a day with God just barely have enough time to clear out their hearts, let alone get any real prayer or communion done. Prayer time with God has many parts. You may be clearing out your heart, making decisions, studying scripture, listening to His Spirit, worshipping, etc., so you need to allow enough time for these different stages with Him.

Let's talk now about why some of these different things are important in the prayer closet.

The bible says to guard our hearts above all things (Proverbs 4:23). So, you need to be spending some time making sure your heart is right before Him. Make sure it is not a spirit of condemnation but rather conviction from the Holy Ghost. As He convicts you, figure out what is going on. Engage in heart healing with Him. Why does this matter? Because if your heart is loud it can make you miss it when giving prophetic words. So clear it out.

Another way you can get words in your private time is just worshipping the Lord. As you focus on Him, He may download a vision or put a word for someone else on your heart.

As you study scripture through the Holy Ghost's promptings, He may give you words through the scriptures for other people.

Warning: Do not pick a random Scripture verse to condemn someone. Always get the Holy Spirit's prompting on a matter.

CHAPTER 9

DELIVERING CORPORATE WORDS

This is one of my favorite things to do, but it is also one of the hardest things to do, as a corporate word affects many people. You have the opportunity to touch a whole people group with the love of God with just one message that is prophetically made for them. It is a beautiful thing. On the flip side, a wrong message can send a whole people group into a spiral. Guard your lips and speak only what the Lord would have you. Do it with fear and trembling for the amount of souls you hold in your hand.

When you pray over a large group, if possible, there should be a lot of intercession over the group beforehand. Pray on behalf of the people there. As you do this, the Lord will start to show you things, and you will start to sense things about the people you are supposed to give the word to. Write these things down, as the devil will try to make you forget what the Lord has told you in the secret place. The more you pray over the people, the more revelation you will get for them. I could probably teach a whole class on this, but I will try to make the most relevant points here.

After you feel the Lord is done downloading the revelations to you, organize them. "Okay Lord, I hear what you want to say to the people, but how do you want to say them? Is there an order? A way? A demonstration that is necessary? How will they understand?" Knowing these things ahead of time will give you a foundation to stand on when it comes time for you to deliver the word. However, let the Holy Ghost interrupt you. I often see two extremes with corporate words being delivered in the prophetic community:

1. People are so stuck to the plan God gave them in secret, that they are not open to additions He may want to make in the moment, and this mourns the Holy Ghost.

2. People have no planning ahead of time and their sermons/corporate words are sloppy. Though they may be anointed, they lack fire and understanding, so though the people feel God move, they aren't sure what the point is and walk away learning nothing.

We must find the balance, as we are called to be prepared in season and out of season. Do your spiritual homework beforehand, and know what God wants to say to the people you are called to.

Another thing to remember is that these are people's hearts you are dealing with. It could be 15 people or 1,500, but their hearts are so important, so do not confuse them from your lack of prayer ahead of time. Give them the word of the Lord as He would have it and do your best to make it make sense to His people.

CHAPTER 10

GROWING IN CONFIDENCE

I could probably write a whole book on this subject, as I have seen so many women and men look at this information, understand it, but never apply it to the fullness God would have them to. Many times when I go up to preach, a spirit of fear tries to jump on my back and make me terrified to preach. "What will they say? What if they don't like it?" These kinds of thoughts go through my head as the spirit of fear tries to stop me from speaking. But I rebuke that spirit, sometimes more than once, and then I go up there and preach. You must rebuke it.

Many men become afraid to share as they worry they will "not have what it takes" and women feel they are "not good enough" to do such things. Neither of these is a Godly thought. If you are saved, Jesus can use you to deliver His prophetic messages, whether corporately or privately. You have to understand that you are going to make some mistakes, and that is okay. You and the Lord can clean them up together. That is all part of the process of this.

A good way to grow prophetic confidence is to start by doing "prophetic tests" on yourself and others.

Here are some things you can do to help your prophetic gift grow in accuracy:

- Ask God to tell you something that is going to happen today. Did it happen? If it did, this will grow your confidence.

- Ask a family member to test out your prophetic gift on them. Ask them if it was accurate. If it was, this will also help your confidence.

- Then maybe try a friend.

- Then maybe try someone at church.

- Then whoever the Lord would say.

I'm sure some of you are worried about what people will say about you if you really decide to walk into the role of prophet or prophetess. The truth is, they may say some bad things. That's just the nature of it. You have to develop a bit of a thick skin if you feel the prophetic is your office. Even if you don't feel called to the office of the prophet, you still may have God prompt you to deliver words. So you need to overcome fear by rebuking it. Remember, fear is a spirit. You need to rebuke that thing and deliver the word of the Lord.

CHAPTER 11

YOU
MATTER

TAKING CARE OF YOURSELF

I have delivered thousands of prophetic words in my ministry. But even before I was officially in ministry, I was prophetically delivering words. Before there was any official ministry, I was delivering words at Walmart, on street corners, small groups, church meetings, etc. I didn't think I needed an official ministry, until one day I realized I was broke. I sat there with around -$200 in my bank account, and could not understand how this could happen. I had made an error with my account by only $1, but was then charged several overdraft fees. I was devastated. I was like, "God, I pray for people all the time. I am always doing your work. How could I be so broke that I am stuck in this mess?" He told me I needed to have a place where people could give to me, as people didn't know they should or could give. So, I created a basic website and started taking up offerings. The overdraft fees were paid by a prophetic girlfriend of mine whose parents felt led to take care of this prophetess.

Why am I telling you this? Because as you start using this gift, people will pull on you and they will want you to use it all the time. But they won't always give back, and you need to take care of your household and yourself. Yes you are a servant of all, but even Jesus pulled away from the people to go pray.

SPIRITUAL ABUSE & BOUNDARIES

I have made some dumb mistakes over the years. After ministry school I was all zealous to prophesy. One night I felt a prompting in my spirit to deliver two messages at a House of Prayer at 2 in the morning. So I rushed there and delivered the two words to two people outside, and then they said "Why don't you come inside, there are others that want words." So they gave me a table (never having met me) and a line started to form. For hours I prophesied over people, prayed for them, and coached them. I really was a blessing to them. But once I had left, I sat in my car and started crying because I was so tired. No one there ever talked to me again, they just used me up and then went on their way.

Some people will use every last drop of you if they can; do not let them. Have boundaries. Say when you are done and what you require. Don't be arrogant, but don't be naive. Some people want to just run to you, take everything from you, and then run away.

I had a guy once who wanted to talk to me for hours, asking me everything. But rarely would he come to my meetings; he just wanted individual attention all the time. Run from these people unless a mentoring relationship has been established. As a prophet, you are not a coke machine that pops out a word every time someone wants one. You are valuable. Though I think we should *never* charge for prophecy, I do think we should accept donations as the Lord leads.

Here is a simple way to stay in peace with the Lord: Just simply ask Him "Should I take up an offering?" Or if someone wants to give you something, see if you have peace about receiving it. Some people will try to give you things with the intention of you becoming their "personal prophet". Is there a hidden motive behind their gift? Identify this with the Lord. Sometimes I have taken gifts and then had to donate them, or in worse cases, trash them, for people may curse items if they had evil intent. This is okay. Do not hold onto gifts just because you feel guilty. It is better to have less than have a house full of demonic items. Live holy.

When you feel spiritually drained, stop. It's ok to tell people no when you are tired and just can't give any more. You could always give them a word later, or someone else could. Or maybe they don't need a word at all, sometimes people need to learn to rely more on God and less on prophets. With someone that is new to the prophetic you may give more, but a seasoned person should need direction less. Listen to the Holy Spirit and use discernment to know which situation is which. Also listen to things that motivate and encourage you, and have others pray for you as well. We should never come to a point where we don't need prayer.

CHAPTER 12

CONCLUSION & SEND OFF

Everyone can prophesy. It might not feel like you can, but you can. If the bible says men and women, young and old, then you can do it! The question is, will you?

We are in a time when many people know what is going on prophetically, but they do not speak up. They say nothing. They are scared to speak. At the same time, some prophetic people are often just talking. Talking about the things they sense God doing, but never trying to implement change.

We need to know what God is saying, speak it out, and walk towards it. Don't be afraid to speak, as the fear of man can bring a snare.

"The fear of man lays a snare, but whoever trusts in the Lord is safe."
Proverbs 29:25 (ESV)

Remember Daniel in the lion's den. He stood for God, but he ended up in a lion's den. But he was unharmed. Often in prophetic ministry the enemy will try and throw you into a lion's den. But there is another group in there. The Holy Spirit, Jesus and Yahweh are in the lion's den with you, and you should not be harmed. As emotionally testing as a lion's den might be, you can come out unharmed. Don't be afraid to speak, as just like Daniel, there is always another side. His open mouth ultimately promoted him.

Trust and speak as He would have you. It might put you in a wilderness or a well or a lion's den, but as Christians we do not die. When you really understand that, fully, you will grow in confidence. We should fear God and want to listen to Him more than we care about what people think.

No matter what comes against you for standing or speaking prophetically for God, there is a due season.

"Whoever welcomes a prophet as a prophet will receive a prophet's reward, and whoever welcomes a righteous person as a righteous person will receive a righteous person's reward."
Matthew 10:41 (NIV)

The first conference I ever spoke at was a father's heart conference in North Carolina. I remember prophesying over this woman about how much the Lord loved her and she flipped out, started crying and rolled herself on the floor. I guess her father was hard and not emotionally sensitive, but she was impacted by the Holy Ghost in that moment, and she said it changed her life. She felt the Lord God as a father for the first time. These moments mark us. I knew I wanted to help people and prophecy has allowed me to do that. It will set a fire in you too. Don't give up on it. When done right, it can help many people.

"Do not despise prophecies."
1 Thessalonians 5:20 (NKJV)

We have to be careful in the prophetic of imaginations. I see way too many people imagining things and thinking it is a "prophetic word" God gave them. If you have a thought to do something, simply submit it to the Holy Spirit. Rather than just assuming it is the Lord, take time to pray.

Be willing to switch things around in the lineup. When you are preaching or teaching or just in your everyday way of life. If the Holy Spirit says I do not want you to go this way or that, listen to Him. Often times when the Holy Spirit starts flowing in a meeting, He doesn't go in the order of the line of people wanting to receive prophetic ministry. I skip people and move around as the Lord wants me to because the anointing has it's own way with people. His ways are not your ways. His thoughts are not your thoughts. Go where the Holy Spirit goes.

SEND OFF

I hope this book helped you understand some of the basic and more complex principles of walking in prophecy. As you embark on this journey, you might make mistakes, and some so wrong that you will question the prophetic all together. Commit now to never give up on it. It is the testimony of Jesus. Like Jeremiah in Jeremiah 20, who questioned his whole ministry and wanted to quit after delivering a word of the Lord, you may ruin into similar times. When you try to take on darkness there will be push back. But you cannot lose faith. You must keep going. Don't make one mistake and say "this prophecy thing isn't for me, I just am not cut out for this." We must continue on the legacy as servants, and some of you as prophets, of the Lord. It is an honor to speak on behalf of the Lord as His trusted mouth piece. We must keep ourselves pure. Though you will never be perfect, we must strive to be better every day, every hour, every year. I know it is worth it, as I have seen the fruit in my life.

Sometimes, if I am honest I question it all because of the push back I have received. But in a brief moment when someone gets a prophetic word through me that changes their lives, I remember it is all worth it. One of my favorite moments of clarity is when I see that a person really heard God through the teachings He gave me. When you see a person healed by your prophetic word... it is all worth it.

The amazing thing about prophecy is that it connects with all the gifts. You can help with anything just because you know Him and what He is saying. Think about it; you have access to a God who has all knowledge and all understanding, so when there is a problem you can find any solution. You must guard your time to protect His gift. It is a hard gift to carry if it is your main one, but you will change people's lives. You get to walk into heaven and know you made a difference. Don't give up on prophecy, you really can change people's lives. Some will not accept this change, but many will.

TIPS TO BECOMING MORE ACCURATE

If you are a leader or want to have a good night with your friends, try prophesying blindfolded. I can't take credit for this idea, I actually learned it from a Pastor in South Carolina. But regardless, here is what you do. You have a group practice prophesying over each other blindfolded.

I did this in my ministry school for several years. I would bring up one of the girls in class and blindfold her, and then I'd have another girl sneak up and stand there silently. Then I'd have the blindfolded girl pray and share what she was feeling from the Lord for that person. It was funny to see all the other girls in class trying not to laugh at how accurate or inaccurate the person was. Then before I had them remove the blindfold, I'd tell them to see if they could hear from the Holy Spirit the name of the person they were prophesying over. Sometimes they would get it right, but often they would not. This was good for them to see where they were at in hearing God.

This is a hard exercise, even for the most seasoned prophets, because there is a lot of pressure on you when you are doing it. Your heart may be loud because you are trying so hard to get specific answers, and there is also the possible embarrassment you may feel, even if it is unwarranted, if you get it wrong. Do not think about trying to get the right answer. Rather, think about communing with God and just wait and listen. Do not allow your mind to think of the others in the room. Just think of your prayer closet and how intimate you are with Him. Let your guard down and allow Him to speak to you, then repeat. We must understand our hearts can be deceitful, and based on the information you receive from the Lord, you may assume it is a specific person in the room. Don't allow yourself to assume anything, just simply listen and repeat.

Why does this matter? Why do a silly activity like this? Because it is going to increase your accuracy, and probably show you some fear of man in your heart. If you miss it, don't assume you are not prophetic. Go home, talk to God about it in your private time with Him, ask Him why you missed it and try it again. When you get it right it is going to feel amazing. We had two girls in our most recent school get it right, and they were so ecstatic. It will feel good, but we have to be careful as prophecy will pass away but love will remain. So don't love getting it right more than Jesus or others, but do rejoice because God is using you.

Kay Note: I normally prophesy with my eyes closed. It is not because I need to per say, it is so I don't get distracted by the things going on around me or by people's reactions. Sometimes people's reactions have nothing to do with the accuracy or inaccuracy of the word. You don't have to do this, but I would suggest it. Many times I open my eyes and see a person crying or laughing. I don't even always know from what part of the word, as I was just focused on giving the word, not on their reaction. If they have a bad reaction, it doesn't necessarily mean that it is wrong. Sometimes it is just something they are dealing with with God, and it has nothing to do with you. So don't get too worked up about it. Even if it is wrong, "I'm sorry" goes a long way with people.

Another tip is to try to be rested. Now I will say that often the night before a prophetic event, especially if it is in the morning, the enemy may try to steal your rest. But honestly, sometimes this works in your favor as you are too tired to think your own thoughts, and so you just repeat what the Lord would say.

Lay off the coffee or caffeine before an event if you get the jitters. I had this friend once who had an amazing prophetic gift, but when they got around the coffee they became inaccurate. Their in-and-out nature in the prophetic kind of kept their ministry from expanding, because people didn't fully trust their words all the time. I do drink tea, but I am almost immune to it at this point. However, I try not to drink it on an empty stomach.

My Secret: I want to tell you a secret. The reason I really believe I was given such a weighty prophetic gift is because of a test that I passed. Before I received my gift, God asked me to do something big... Give up all my stuff and follow Him. It was one of the hardest things I've ever done. But this testing and ridding my house of demonic things led me into a high level of accuracy. I also have an open hand, and will get rid of pretty much anything the Lord asks me to (though I did hide a pair of heels from Him once several years ago... I did eventually get rid of them though). We have to have open hands and open hearts in the prophetic. It will help you have less noise, and with less noise comes more accuracy. Let it go. All of it. Then see the Lord move. Just give it to Him. I promise, there is another side. I wish someone would have told me that. I thought I would be a vagabond for the rest of my life, living in a tent owning one outfit. But it was a test. God had far more for me. There is a cost to having a gift, but if you will pay it, you will be rewarded.

I hope you enjoyed this book and feel a new fire for the prophetic. May you bless many people with this gift and train others to prophesy as well, as it edifies the body and helps us all stay encouraged as we walk in our calls from Him.

ABOUT THE AUTHOR

Kay Nash is a messenger and prophetess of the Lord who prophesies in the U.S. and internationally. She holds a Bachelor's Degree in Radio and Television Broadcast from the University of Central Florida, and is a former Christian Television Producer. Kay is known for her sensitivity to the Holy Spirit and her accuracy in the prophetic. She spends her time helping women to hear the Lord's voice well and walk more fully in their destiny. Kay also speaks at conferences to equip women more in the word of God.

For more info on Kay's ministry, including training videos, her itinerary, and booking information, please visit:

www.KayNashMinistries.com